Naughty Word of the Day

365 days of slang and swear words for adults

Tamara L Adams

Thank you for your purchase!!
I hope you enjoy!!

If you leave a review on Amazon, let me know via email or social media and I'll send you a free book of your choice from my collection on Amazon!

tamaraadamsauthor@gmail.com

www.tamaraladamsauthor.com

https://twitter.com/@TamaraLAdams

https://www.facebook.com/TamaraLAdamsAuthor/

http://www.amazon.com/T.L.-Adams/e/B00YSROGC4

Have Fun :)

Here is a fun word for each day of the year.

Try to use it in a sentence for more fun!

Day 1:

Knob head - British slang word that translates to dick head.

Day 2:

Piss flaps - Dangly Vaginal Lips.

Day 3:

Twat - Slang word for a vagina.

Day 4:

Shitbag - A very lazy person who deceptively hides their lack of work or effort.

Day 5:

Cocknose - Rub a dick with your nose.

Day 6:

Dickweed - A completely self-absorbed, useless asshole with shit for brains.

Day 7:

Bitch tits – Male breasts or man-boobs.

Day 8:

Arsebadger - An individual who causes painful levels of discomfort.

Day 9:

Jizz cock - Insult thought of by Mark on the television show <u>Peep Show</u>.

Day 10:

Wanker - Someone who is a useless inefficient time-waster.

Day 11:

Bollocks - A term of exasperation at having made a big damn mistake.

Day 12:

Fuck bucket - A complete and utter idiot who annoys you constantly.

Day 13:

Damn - An expression of complete dismay.

Day 14:

Prick - A guy who thinks he knows everything but in reality is a stupid hypocrite.

Day 15:

Shit pouch - Another name for a sassy mouth that a shit load of crap comes out of.

Day 16:

Fucker – One who is rude, obnoxious or just plain mean.

Day 17:

Jizz stain – When a guy jacks off and gets semen on fabric such as a shirt.

Day 18:

Ass – a foolish, stupid person.

Day 19:

Piss wizard – Name coined by the Twitter Universe

Day 20:

Cunt puddle - A pool of juice at the base of a girls feet when she becomes highly aroused.

Day 21:

Dickweasel - A person who is totally rude and not trustworthy.

Day 22:

Fanny flaps – A British word used to refer to a woman's vaginal lips.

Day 23:

Twatface - A terrible politician.

Day 24:

Fucknugget - An insult for someone you find a complete nugget of fucks.

Day 25:

Crap - What one says when they are afraid to say shit.

Day 26:

Arsehole – An annoying person you'd love to smack the crap out of.

Day 27:

Dickhead - A person who shows all to well they are an idiot.

Day 28:

Shit magnet - Person who seems to attract terrible things and events to them.

Day 29:

Bitch - A word used to express a multitude of strong emotions.

Day 30:

Bumhole - A hole between your butt cheeks.

Day 31:

Shite - A very British and therefore great way of saying shit.

Day32:

Scrote – A person who is less than a scrotum.

Day 33:

Cuntflaps – The two outer folds of the vulva.

Day 34:

Fuckwit – A person who is not only lacking in clue but is apparently unable to get clue even when handed to them on a plate.

Day 35:

Arsebastard – Some one who is an arse and a bastard, so therefore an arse bastard.

Day 36:

Wankface - A complete and total two faced, wanker, bastard.

Day 37:

Shithouse - Someone who is the epitome of scum or the lowest of all lows.

Day 38:

Knobcheese - Smegma secreted/collected between the penis and foreskin.

Day 39:

Jizzbreath - Breath of a person who just finished blowing a guy

Day 40:

Piss artist - Someone who can down 24 beers and carry on like a champ.

Day 41:

Cock - The male reproductive organ or a secondary brain.

Day 42:

Nutsack - A stupid fucker who does or says dumb shit and will not stop.

Day 43:

Stiffie - An erection of the penis.

Day 44:

Fuck-face ~ Someone acting like a bitch.

Day 45:

Choad ~ Having a penis that is wider than it is long.

Day 46:

Clusterfuck ~ A huge problem or situation.

Day 47:

Shitlist ~ A number of persons who you strongly disapprove of.

Day 48:

Assclown - Someone who doesn't know what the hell they are talking about and has no idea that everyone talks shit about them.

Day 49:

Fuckstick - An idiot.

Day 50:

Asshole - An inconsiderate, arrogant, uncaring, selfish, spiteful, bastard of a man.

Day 51:

Peckerhead - One who has a penis for brains with no social skills.

Day 52:

Rimjob – Kissing or licking someone's asshole.

Day 53:

Shit cunt – An Australian term for the lowest level of insult of which one can receive.

Day 54:

Jizzmuffin - When you cum in muffin mix, bake them and then give them away.

Day 55:

Shitspitter – A nonsensical person who tries to talk shit.

Day 56:

Cock Tease ~ A person who flirts and seduces men without engaging in sex.

Day 57:

Wingnut ~ An eccentric person.

Day 58:

Buttmunch ~ Seemingly derogatory term but often used with affection toward a sibling.

Day 59:

Shitlicker ~ A derogatory term for a person you could think of as actually licking shit.

Day 60:

Dickbag – A combination of douchebag and Dickhead.

Day 61:

Asshat – One who has their head up their ass. Therefor wearing their ass as a hat.

Day 62:

Dickweed – A self absorbed asshole with shit for brains.

Day 63:

Dumbfuck – Someone who does not know what a dumbfuck is or that they are one.

Day 64:

Lame ass - A person that is being a bastard or boring and knows it.

Day 65:

Shittiest – The worst of the worst possible shit.

Day 66:

Fuck - The only fucking word that can be put everyfuckinghwere and still fucking make fucking sense.

Day 67:

Shit - Feces. Poop. Dookie. Poo Poo.

Day 68:

Douche – Between an ass hole and a jerk.

Day 69:

Bumblefuck – The damn middle of fucking nowhere.

Day 70:

Cockwomble - A completely useless person who talks bullshit all the damn time.

Day 71:

Bollock face – A person who's face looks like a man's ball sack.

Day 72:

Shitnuggit - Someone who is full of shit.

Day 73:

Thundercunt - The worst level of cunt you can possibly get.

Day 74:

Asswipe - A stupid and annoying person.

Day 75:

Cumbubble - A person who burps up a bubble of cum after a blowjob.

Day 76:

Douchecanoe ~ A boat used by douches to move around a conversation to spread their message of doucheness to others.

Day 77:

Dildo ~ A Damn Plastic Penis!

Day 78:

Boner ~ When a guy's dick thinks your cute and say's hi.

Day 79:

Chogasm ~ An orgasm from a very thick but short penis.

Day 80:

Dumbass - The biggest idiot of all idiots.

Day 81:

Fuckboy - Asshole boy who will lead a girl on only to let her down, then apologize only to then let her down again.

Day 82:

Fugly - Fucking ugly.

Day 83:

Fuckgirl - A girl who thinks they are god's gift to men but only leads them on.

Day 84:

Fuckstick – A huge idiot.

Day 85:

Shitty – Worthless or resembling shit.

Day 86:

Beauty box – Female vagina.

Day 87:

Gooch – The area between ass and your balls.

Day 88:

Hummer ~ More than a blowjob; it's when a person actually hums when their mouth is around your penis or balls.

Day 89:

Hump ~ To grind your genitals against someone or something.

Day 90:

Krunk ~ Derived from the two words: "crazy drunk".

Day 91:

Skeet ~ The act of ejaculation.

Day 92:

Lil rat – An annoying little shit who shows off and always stirs up shit.

Day 93:

Orgasm - A climax of sexual excitement, characterized by feelings of pleasure centered in the genitals.

Day 94:

Shizzum - A combination of the word shit and jizzum.

Day 95:

Snipe - A very attractive girl.

Day 96:

Skank – A slutty person who doesn't know how to say no to sex.

Day 97:

Skooger – A male cougar who has sexual relations with a younger female.

Day 98:

Fuckchodi – Intensely annoying or stupid event/statement.

Day 99:

Splooge – An ejaculation deposit.

Day 100:

Fuck – Sex, or an Intensifier

Day 101:

Bellend – Head of the penis.

Day 102:

Shitfaced – Stupidly drunk.

Day 103:

Balls – Testicles

Day 104:

Badass - Someone ready to cause trouble.

Day 105:

Ballsy - A aggressively tough.

Day 106:
Chickenshit - One who is super wussy.

Day 107:

Bazooms - A woman's breasts

Day 108:

Dipshit - A foolish or contemptible person.

Day 109:

Hardass - A person who strictly enforces rules.

Day 110:

Blowjob - Sucking on someones penis.

Day 111:

Boody - The buttocks.

Day 112:

Cojones - Testicles

Day 113:
Boink - To have sexual intercourse.

Day 114:
Bullshit - To talk foolishly or boastfully.

Day 115:

Cocksucker - A complete asshole.

Day 116:

Crapper – When something is super terrible.

Day 117:

Piss Off – Leave me alone.

Day 118:

Shoot the Shit – Talk about nothing.

Day 119:

Johnson – Slang for penis.

Day 120:

Fucker – A terrible person you hate.

Day 121:

Shithead – A foolish, inept person.

Day 122:
Goddamn – An exclamation of any strong feeling, especially disgust or irritation.

Day 123:

Nooky – Fun sexual intercourse.

Day 124:

Wank – To masturbate.

Day 125:

Horseshit – It's like bullshit but with more attitude.

Day 126:

Motherfucker – A despicable or very unpleasant person or thing.

Day 127:
Pisser – Something extremely disagreeable.

Day 128:

Cunt - The most vulgar term for a vagina.

Day 129:
Shitless - Extremely frightened.

Day 130:

Wazoo - The anus.

Day 131:

Spaz - Clumsy, foolish, incompetent person.

Day 132:

Cockburger - Somebody who is arrogant and flaunts it.

Day 133:

Bastard - An insult to someone whose parents ain't married.

Day 134:
Shitload - A large amount.

Day 135:

Fubar - Fucked up beyond all repair.

Day 136:
Willie - The penis.

Day 137:

Arse - A stupid, irritating person.

Day 138:

Bugger - Used to express emotion when making a mistake.

Day 139:

Minger - An unattractive or unpleasant person or thing.

Day 140:

Sod-off – Telling someone to go away.

Day 141:

Son of a bitch – A scoundrel or thoroughly disagreeable person.

Day 142:

Tits – Vulgar word for breasts.

Day 143:

Pissed Off – So very angry.

Day 144:

Cougar – An older woman who sleeps with a younger man.

Day 145:

Bellend – An annoying or contemptible man.

Day 146:

Fanny Flaps – Someones fat ass.

Day 147:

Knob – An obnoxious person.

Day 148:

Snatch – The second most horrific sounding nickname for a female's genitals.

Day 149:

Beef Curtains – The cruel term for long, hanging inner labia.

Day 150:

Fap – A representation of masturbation often used online.

Day 151:

Sporking – Spooning with an erection.

Day 152:

Dick Inches - Arbitrary unit of measurement used by men when overestimating the size of their dicks.

Day 153:

Fling Cleaning - The act of tidying your room before a date in case you get laid later.

Day 154:

Masturnap - Falling asleep after masturbating.

Day 155:

Manther - Male cougar.

Day 156:

Pornocchio - A person who embellishes their sex life in order to sound cooler.

Day 157:

Sexorcism - Sleeping with someone new to get over an ex.

Day 158:

FuckIt List - A list of people you hope to bang before you die.

Day 159:

Condomplate - To contemplate the uses of a condom.

Day 160:

Jackintosh - A computer used exclusively for pornographic.

Day 161:

Procrasturbating - Using masturbation to avoid more pressing matters.

Day 162:

Screwvenir - A small souvenir taken from a lover following sexual encounter.

Day 163:

Dick - Someone who is a complete asshole.

Day 164:

Bareback - Sex without a condom.

Day 165:

Teabagging - Slang term for the sexual act of a man placing his scrotum in the mouth or onto the head of his partner for pleasure.

Day 166:

Cockblock - An intentional act that serves to prevent someone from having sex.

Day 167:

Quickie - A brief act of sexual intercourse.

Day 168:

Mile High Club – Having sex in an airplane while in flight.

Day 169:

Climax – Culmination of an amazing sexual act.

Day 170:

One Night Stand – Two people have sex only once and have no relationship.

Day 171:

Potency – The physical ability of a man to have sex.

Day 172:

Nookie – Fun sex.

Day 173 –

Threesome – Three people having sex.

Day 174:

Bull Fucker – One who bullshits heavily.

Day 175:

Dickwad – A person who is just an asshole all the time.

Day 176:

Cunt Lapper – A step up from asshole but worse than a douchebag.

Day 177:

Stankin Ass Bitch – Worst form of a woman you can be to another.

Day 178:

Dick Lips – A woman with full lips.

Day 179:

What the hell? – Screamed in annoyance at someone who does something stupid.

Day 180:

Kiss My Ass – The best possible way to tell someone no or to go away.

Day 181:

Fucking Shit – What to say when you are angry at at a loss for words.

Irish Dirty Words

Day 182:

Gobdaw – A gullible idiot.

Day 183:

Fecker – A mild form of fucker.

Day 184:

Ráicleach – A loose woman.

Day 185:

Cúl Tóna – Dickhead

Day 186:

Aiteann – Translates to cunt.

Day 187:

Téigh go dtí ifreann! – Go to hell.

Day 188:

Póg mo thóin. – Kiss My Ass.

Day 189:

Gombeen – Small time loser wheeler and dealer.

Day 190:

Gobshite – Loud mouthed person who talks a lot about nothing of value.

Day 191:

Scut – A Super useless person.

Day 192:

Wagon – Someone with fat ass.

Day 193:

Dryshite – Boring, unspontaneous person.

Day 194:

Gowl – Slang for pussy/vagina.

Day 195:

Eejit – Slang term for someone who acts foolishly.

Day 196:

Tool – Someone who acts like a dick, because...well...he's compensating.

Day 197:

Geebag – Foolish person.

Day 198:

Bollix – Unpleasant jerk of a person.

French Dirty Words

Day 199:

Merde ~ Shit

Day 200:

Putain ~ Whore

Day 201:

C'est des Conneries ~ This is Bullshit.

Day 202:

Salope ~ Bitch

Day 203:

Fils de Salope – Son of a Bitch.

Day204:

T'as Pas de Couilles – You Don't Have the Balls.

Day 205:

Je M'en Fous – I Don't Give a Shit.

Day 206:

Osti de Calisse de Tabarnak (Quebec only) – Goddamn Motherfucking Shit!

Day 207:

Zut – Darn or shoot.

Day 208:

Fais Chier – That pisses me off.

Day 209:

Connard – Asshole or bitch.

Day 210:

Casse-toi – Fuck off.

Day 211:

Ta gueule - Shut the fuck up.

Day 212:

Nique Ta Mere - Fuck your mother.

Day 213:

Cul - Ass

Spanish Dirty Words

Day 214:

Mierda – Bullshit

Day 215:

Váyase a la Mierda – Fuck off.

Day 216:

Que te Folle un Pez – I Hope You Get Fucked By a Fish.

Day 217:

Puto – Fucking

Day 218:

Verga – Cock or Prick

Day 219:

Cojones – Balls

Day 220:

Coño – Cunt

Day 221:

Joder – Fuck

Day 222:

Carajo – Damn it.

Day 223:

Idiota – Dumbass

Day 224:

Hijo de Puta – Son of a bitch.

Day 225:

Estupido – Douchebag

Day 226:

Pendejo – Asshole

Day 227:

Zorra - Bitch

Day 228:

Mericon – Pussy

Day 229:

Mamon – Prick

Day 230:

Maltido – Damn

Day 231:

Tarado – Moron

Day 232:

Gilipollas – Shithead

Day 233:

Cabrón – Asshat

Day 234:

Tonto del culo – An idiot of the ass.

Day 235:

Puta madre – Motherfucker

Day 236:

Vete al Demonio – Go to hell.

Day 237:

Que te jodan – Fuck you.

Day 238:

Que te den — Up yours.

Italian Dirty Words

Day 239:

Cazzo – Fuck

Day 240:

Che Palle! – What balls!

Day 241:

Tette – Tits

Day 242:

Stronzo – Asshole

Day 243:

Che cazzo – What the Fuck.

Day 244:

Fongoul – Fuck You.

Day 245:

Pompinara – Cocksucker

Day 246:

A fanabla – Go to hell.

Day 247:

Bacha ma culo ~ Kiss my ass.

Day 248:

Cazzata - Bullshit

Day 249:

Dio cane! ~ Fucking god.

Day 250:

Figlio di Troia ~ Son of a Bitch.

Day 251:

Leccaculo – Kiss my ass.

Day 252:

Mafankulo – Motherfucker

Day 253:

Pezzo di merda – Piece of shit.

Day 254:

Porca troia – Fucking hell.

Day 255:

Segaiolo – Wanker

Day 256:

Sfacim e merde – Fucking Shit.

Day 257:

Sti cazza – Fuck that.

Day 258:

Testa di cazzo – Dickhead

Day 259:

Un pompino ~ Blowjob

Day 260:

Vai all'inferno ~ Go to hell.

Day 261:

Zuia ~ Bitch

Day 262:

Bastardo ~ Bastard

Day 263:

Cazzo sí – Fuck you!

Day 264:

Scopare – To have sex.

German Dirty Words

Day 265:

Arschgesicht – Ass Face.

Day 266:

Küss Meinen Arsch – Kiss My Ass.

Day 267:

Verpiss Dich! – Fuck Off!

Day 268:

Zur Hölle Mit ihnen – To hell with em.

Day 269:

Wichser – Wanker

Day 270:

Arschgeige – Dickhead

Day 271:

Verdammt! – Damn!/Dammit

Day 272:

Sheisse – Shit

Day 273:

Sohn einer Hündin! – Son of a bitch!

Day 274:

Der Mist – This shit.

Day 275:

Was zur Hölle? – What the hell?

Day 276:

Depp – Idiot

Day 277:

Arschloch – Asshole

Day 278:

Miststück – Bitch

Day 279:

Du Bastard! – Bastard!

Day 280:

Fick dich – Fuck you!

Day 281:

Dummkopf – Shithead

Day 282:

Flachwichser – Fuckwit

Portuguese Dirty Words

Day 283:

Cabra – Bastard or Fucker

Day 284:

Monte de Merda – Piece of Shit.

Day 285:

Caralho – Dick

Day 286:

Vai Para o Caralho – Go Fuck Yourself.

Day 287:

Rego Do Cu – Ass Crack.

Day 288:

Puta Que Pariu – Holy Shit.

Day 289:

Chupa-mos – Suck it

Day 290:

Merda – Shit

Day 291:

Filho da mãe – Son of a Bitch.

Day 292:

Corno – Fool

Day 293:

Vai tomar no cu! – Up yours!

Day 294:

Puta merda – Holy shit.

Day 295:

Nem fodendo – No fucking way.

Day 296:

Que porra é essa? – What the fuck?

Day 297:

Arrombado – Sucker

Day 298:

Fodido – Fucked

Russian Swear Words

Day 299:

Khui – Dick

Day 300:

Khui tebé! – Fuck You!

Day 301:

Suchka – Little Bitch

Day 302:

Obosrat'sya – Crapping One's Pants.

Day 303:

Ne bud' zhopoy! – Don't Be an Asshole!

Day 304:

Blyad' – Whore

Day 305:

Da yebal ya eto! – I Fucked Up!

Day 306:

Svo-lach' – Jerk

Day 307:

Piz-dets – Damn it

Day 308:

Hui – Dick

Day 309:

Mu-dak- Shithead

Day 310:

Zho-pa – Arse

Day 311:

Ye-bat' ~ Fuck

Day 312:

Su-ka ~ Bitch

Day 313:

Gav-no ~ Shit

Day 314:

Blyat' ~ Whore

Chinese Swear Words

Day 315:

Wáng Bā Dàn ~ Tortoise Egg.

Day 316:

Gǒu Pì ~ That's bullshit.

Day 317:

Hùn zhàng ~ Git/Bastard

Day 318:

Tā mā de ~ Fuck

Day 319:

Qù nǐ de ~ Shut the Fuck Up.

Day 320:

Wǒ Cào ~ Holy Shit

Day 321:

Hún dàn ~ Bastard

Day 322:

Níúbì ~ Fucking Awesome

Day 323:

Gǔnkāi – Go to hell.

Day 324:

Diǎo sī – Loser

Day 325:

Gàn – Fuck

Day 326:

Hùnzhàng – Bullshit

Day 327:

Cào nǐ mā ~ Motherfucker

Japanese Swear Words

Day 328:

Kuso – Shit/Damn/Fuck

Day 329:

Yariman – Slut

Day 330:

Kusottare – Shithead

Day 331:

Busu – Ugly Hag.

Day 332:

Shi'ne – Go to hell.

Day 333:

Kutabare, boke – Fuck Off, You piece of shit.

Day 334:

Baka – Stupid

Day 335:

Uzai – Pain in the ass.

Day 336:

Chikushō – Oh Shit!

Day 337:

Bakayarou – Asshole

Day 338:

Shinjimae – Go to hell.

Day 339:

Chikushou – Son of a bitch.

Day 340:

Kutabare – Fuck you.

Day 341:

Yariman – Slut

Korean Dirty Words

Day 342:

Ah, Sshi-bal – Ah, Fuck.

Day 343:

Sshi-bang-sae – Fuck You.

Day 344:

Byung-shin-a! - You Dumbass!

Day 345:

Gae-sae – Son of a bitch.

Day 346:

Nyeon – Bitch

Day 347:

Jot – Penis/Dick/Cock

Day 348:

Jeot-gat-eun-nom/nyeon – You bastard/bitch.

Day 349:

Nyeon – Bitch

Day 350:

Nom – Bastard

Day 351:

Gae-sae-ggi – Son of a bitch!

Day 352:

Jae-gi-ral – Damn it!

Day 353:

Jaen-jang – Shit

Hindi Swear Words

Day 354:

Chutiya chootia ~ Fucker

Day 355:

Gaand chaat mera ~ Kiss my ass

Day 356:

Gaandu ~ Asshole

Day 357:

Kaminey ~ Bastard

Day 358:

Lund Khajoor - Dickhead

Day 359:

Mader chod – Motherfucker

Day 360:

Mera mume le – Suck my dick

Day 361:

Chod - Fuck

Day 362:

Chootia - Dumbass

Day 363:

Chutiya - Wanker

Day 364:

Kutte ki olad - Son of a bitch

Day 365:

Ja gand mara - Go get fucked

Books by Tamara L Adams

Angry Journal
Art Up This Journal
Backstabbing Bitches: Adult Activities
Puptivities: Adult Activities
Cativities: Adult Activities
Activititties: Adult Activities
I Hate My Boss: Adult Activities
Activity Book for Adults
Activity Book You Never Knew You Wanted But Can't Live Without
Activity Book You need to Buy Before You Die
Fuck I'm Bored : Adult Activity Book
I'm Still Fucking Bored
The Activity Book That Will Transform Your Life
Activities to do while you number two
Timmy and the Dragon
Unmotivated Coloring
Angry Coloring
Coloring Happy Quotes
Inspirational Quotes Coloring
Coloring Cocktails
Cussing Creatures Color
101 Quote Inspired Journal Prompts
Unlocking Happiness Planner
Daily Fitness Planner
Bloggers Daily Planner
Bloggers Daily Planner w margins
Writers Daily Planner
Writers Daily Planner w coloring
Busy Mothers Planner
Where's Woody Coloring Book
99 Writing Prompts
Deciding Destiny: Lindsays Choice
Rich Stryker: Julie's Last Hope
Rich Stryker: Tom's Final Justice
Unlocking Happiness
Getting to Know Yourself Journal

Printed in Great Britain
by Amazon

85561110R00057